Some Other Where

Steven Matthews is a poet and critic from Colchester, Essex. He was an inaugural poet in residence at the Natural History Museum, Oxford, in 2015–16. His previous poetry collections are *Skying* (Waterloo Press, 2012) and *On Magnetism* (Two Rivers Press, 2017). A selection of his museum poetry was included in the anthology *Guests of Time* (Valley Press, 2017).

Some Other Where

Steven Matthews

By the same author

On Magnetism (Two Rivers Press, 2017)
Skying (Waterloo Press, 2012)

Also by Two Rivers Poets

David Attwooll, *The Sound Ladder* (2015)
Charles Baudelaire, *Paris Scenes* translated by Ian Brinton (2021)
William Bedford, *The Dancers of Colbek* (2020)
Kate Behrens, *Man with Bombe Alaska* (2016)
Kate Behrens, *Penumbra* (2019)
Kate Behrens, *Transitional Spaces* (2022)
Conor Carville, *English Martyrs* (2019)
David Cooke, *A Murmuration* (2015)
David Cooke, *Sicilian Elephants* (2021)
Tim Dooley, *Discoveries* (2022)
Jane Draycott, *Tideway* (re-issued 2022)
Claire Dyer, *Interference Effects* (2016)
Claire Dyer, *Yield* (2021)
John Froy, *Sandpaper & Seahorses* (2018)
James Harpur, *The Examined Life* (2021)
Maria Teresa Horta, *Point of Honour* translated by Lesley Saunders (2019)
Ian House, *Just a Moment* (2020)
Gill Learner, *Chill Factor* (2016)
Gill Learner, *Change* (2021)
Sue Leigh, *Chosen Hill* (2018)
Sue Leigh, *Her Orchards* (2021)
Becci Louise, *Octopus Medicine* (2017)
Mairi MacInnes, *Amazing Memories of Childhood, etc.* (2016)
Steven Matthews, *On Magnetism* (2017)
Henri Michaux, *Storms under the Skin* translated by Jane Draycott (2017)
René Noyau, *Earth on Fire and other Poems* translated by Gérard Noyau
    with Peter Pegnall (2021)
James Peake, *Reaction Time of Glass* (2019)
James Peake, *The Star in the Branches* (2022)

Peter Robinson & David Inshaw, *Bonjour Mr Inshaw* (2020)
Peter Robinson, *English Nettles* (re-issued 2022)
Lesley Saunders, *Nominy-Dominy* (2018)
Lesley Saunders, *This Thing of Blood & Love* (2022)
Jack Thacker, *Handling* (2018)
Susan Utting, *Half the Human Race* (2017)
Jean Watkins, *Precarious Lives* (2018)

First published in the UK in 2023 by Two Rivers Press
7 Denmark Road, Reading RG1 5PA.
www.tworiverspress.com

© Steven Matthews 2023

The right of the poet to be identified as the author of this work
has been asserted by him in accordance with the Copyright, Designs
and Patents Act of 1988.

All rights reserved. No part of this publication may be reproduced,
stored in or introduced into a retrieval system, or transmitted,
in any form, or by any means (electronic, mechanical, photocopying,
recording or otherwise) without the prior written permission
of the publisher.

ISBN 978-1-915048-06-6

1 2 3 4 5 6 7 8 9

Two Rivers Press is represented in the UK by Inpress Ltd
and distributed by Ingram Publisher Services UK.

Cover illustration and design by Sally Castle
Text design by Nadja Guggi and typeset in Janson and Parisine

Printed and bound in Great Britain by Severn, Gloucester

Acknowledgements

Acknowledgements are due to the following publications, where earlier versions of some of the poems in this collection first appeared: *Axon Magazine*, *Ceaseless Music* (Bloomsbury), *Guests of Time* edited by John Holmes (Valley Press), *London Magazine*, *Metamorphic: 21st Century Poets Respond to Ovid* edited by Nessa O'Mahony and Paul Munden (Recent Work Press), *Poetry Salzburg Review*, *Rebel Talk* edited by Rip Bulkeley, and *Stand Magazine*.

'Yet With Time's Cycles Forests Swell' was set as the final part of a song cycle for soprano and string quartet by Cheryl Frances-Hoad, *Those Endless Forms Most Beautiful*, which was premiered in October 2019.

For Elleke, Thomas, and Sam, with love

Contents

I.

Handing Back the Key | 2
You Ghosted Me | 3
Homages | 4
Sounding the Light and the Land | 7
Laths | 9
Vertigo on Your Birthday Trip to Tintern | 12
Ladders | 14
Riverrun, Cockermouth | 15
July 20th 1969 | 17
Friday Woods | 18
From a Canal Bench | 19
Red Mason Bee | 20
Stag Beetles | 21
Kites at Wittenham Clumps | 22
Medusas | 23
Away | 24
'Yet With Time's Cycles Forests Swell' | 25
The Dying of Orpheus | 27
Dedham Vale | 29
Some Other Where | 30

II. The Valley of the Temples: *A Fantasia*

Elements | 36
Agrigento, Sicily | 38
Hera | 41
Concordia | 45
Herakles | 50
Castor and Pollux | 54
The Chthonic Gods and Demeter's Spring | 58
Recognition | 64
The Way Across | 65

'Tut, I have lost my selfe; I am not here'
— *Romeo and Juliet*, I, I, 192–3

I.

Handing Back the Key

By the time you got the key to that door
back to me, the door itself had vanished
together with the keyhole, hinges, wall –
all of it rubbished to open the space
for the humming new glass-framed offices.

Now I shift on that brass key from jacket
to jacket, and grasp hold of it entering
into empty rooms or walking bridges,
in case one time I need it to open
some lock in the air, and step across.

You Ghosted Me

with silence,
your turning away,

shadow from presence
never now to be.

I transmit all I am
into spaces

where you are not

    *

Sometimes you, mirageously there
in a different form,
like and unlike;

light investing
hair, skin, bones,
your whole body

doubling,
yourself and another's:
thoughts, dreams,

desire-particles flowing
between us
ours and not-ours

Homages

I.

Sound II
(Anthony Gormley)

I am the cast black bowl
with water reflecting
his bowed head; he gentles

me in his prayerful
hands as he gazes
downward, wondering at

the cupped limpid
liquid which yet
gives him back

to himself, as
he is echoed
up to his thighs

in the arch-shadowed
cryptal waters
that resonate

him into
shifting deeps
silent-standing

II.

The Grave-Tender
(Thomas Hardy)

Autumn wind thrashes yew branches
hanging over family graves.

He kneels, trousers staining with mulch,
bald old man intent at his task,

his liver-stained fingers taking
on the strain, clasping at this grave's

crumbling, name-cancelling, headstone.
With the scraper he's carved, knot-hard

ash-wood, he scrapes vigorously at
granite's ingrown moss of the years.

III.

Cantus
(Arvo Part)

The aircraft hanger hushed,
the baby in its carriage lulled,
the short line
of coated and muffled
people with suitcases stilled
when the uniformed officer
eased down the button
on the cassette machine,
and the toothed
spools turned, releasing

the *Cantus* into
that wide emptiness –
its tolls, string ascents and descents
flying waveringly out,
scaled to cross
the gaps between

taevas and lands,
silver-headed star-nails
and trees

Sounding the Light and the Land

Upper Bockhampton and Max Gate

I.

The four-year-old waits, sat upon the stairs,
his eyes fixed on the wall's Venetian red,
watching chromatics of light at sunset.
In Spring or Autumn, light intensifies,
sets colours' embers glowing a short while
before it slips away, leaving a dim
aftermath framed in its decline below
window-level. Tensed, scarcely able to
utter through his melancholy, the boy
recites *And now another day is gone*
to himself, to the last light, to his hopes,
then climbs his now cheerful heart to sleep.

II.

The teenaged boy scuffles the dense carpet
of fallen red and yellow leaves in the wood.
Coppices of larch and ash, yew and pine.
He rakes together heaps, throws flames in handfuls
from slippery rises by the Roman Road.
Light moves. The sunlight clears a wide path
through the newly stark branches. He stops his game,
unfurls drying chestnut fans, stoops to choose
a thin stick to take in hand, peel its bark.
He kneels at the edge of a muddy puddle,
gently dips in the stick, writes words across
the leaves' veins, making fragile notes of them.

III.

When labourers dig out the house foundations
the shovels and mattocks strike against chalk
and yellowed bones appear laid on the white stone.
They kneel with sharp trowels and paint brushes,
work for hours with tensed breaths, unearthing
three hunched, agelessly perfect skeletons:
their arced spines, knees pulled in to the jaws' base,
make them seem, he will write, *like chicks in shells*.

IV.

In each of his writing rooms, the complex
mullions and bars of the window-frames
he designed so *each should be just that way*
see light scribbling on the walls. Tree-shadows
shimmer on matte against iridescence;
the sounds of the winds are shut out from his silence.
Through each day, dark skeins thicken, brights hazing.

V.

More years pass, more excavations to build
the towering red bricked wings of this last house.
He grabs a crowbar alongside the workmen,
drives it into the soil, seeking purchase
beneath the henge of heavy, shaped, sandstone,
straining through the day to set it upright,
a struggle *like the raising of Babel*.
His unmorticed study panes catch glances
as they take into themselves dying suns.

Laths

A Country Revealed
after Bonnefoy

A star on the threshold;
wind, gripped
in still hands.

Words and wind
tussled for ages,
then wind-quiet
fell with a shock.

The country discovered
was merely grey stone:
a way off and far below,
the light from void
streams was laid out.

Night-rains shocked
the earth, unveiled
that fire you call time.

*

the quick feints
and sharp skirmishes
of a ghost lemur
skittering the canopy,
fleeting through;

in a flurry of sunlight
across the city street,
the back of that head,
that swift jittering stride
as though his

*

birdsong let through
windows, vertiginous
prospect, soft breaths
as over
mountainsides,

or over a hillside
from a tiled open room,
geometric mosaics;
your hands cool
as chorusing waters
beneath our blue cupola
with painted stars

*

raddle of sunlight
washes across
groups statuing
the shore
(mount of black clouds
beyond its reach),

sounds shredded
between them as they lean
into the wind,
fostered
in what
they strain to hear

before it is lost
to them,
that day
of two rainbows

*

are the handprints
on granite,
ash, ochre,
reddle, dust,
by those
pressing from
cave side in,

or those from
inside the rock
yearning out

*

Delphi on the Second Day
after Bonnefoy

*Here the troubled voice
consents to love
simple stone,
flagstones time has
enslaved and freed,
the olive-tree, whose strength
is the tang of dry stone.*

*A footstep in a true place:
the fraught voice
now happy beneath silent
rock-slopes, and the infinite,
indefinite answer
from small bells, the shore,
or death. Delphi,
on that second day,
your cloudless valley
struck no terror.*

Vertigo on Your Birthday Trip to Tintern

The land was sodden; our walk across the Wye
via the Mill Bridge was slow and slippery.
The steep woods dripped overnight rain from leaves
turning orange, red, beige towards winter.
The green river swelled, raced beneath the bridge
a rushing devastation; the silence
in the valley was interrupted by
the drone of chain-saws thinning the tree-steads,
persistent ghost-voices from summer's bees.
Shouts of fans and footballers shivered nerves
when they broke from the pitch beside ruins
in a field outside the Abbey's fenced bounds.
Looked back to, fractured slate-grey walls, empty
windows framed a threatening sky. The clouds,
static, seemed drawn down to the river's thread.

Brown mud stood thick on the pathway upward
through the weeping woods, towards a rampart –
the broken leaf-strewn mound of Offa's dyke
on top of the hillside. We slithered on,
grabbing at springy saplings for balance,
determined to achieve high perspectives
on the ancient buildings, the scope of land,
and the tree-line's ridge beyond, into hills
like ripples resonating from this source.

Then, suddenly, we came upon a small,
flat plateau, the mud shelving steeply down
opening into a stark drop. Trailing
at the back of our group, knees giving way,
mind reeling forward into the valley,
embedded shale dislodging and skiting,
my nerves teetered at the brink of cascade,
shoes starting to lose grip, skid on the edge.

I could neither turn on myself nor step
out across the open slide to safety
amongst the dense trees four yards ahead.
As I crouched to the ground, to clasp fingers
into the unsustaining mud, your firm hand
under my elbow drew me back upright
and along the dangerous path, the view
down across to the Abbey steadying now,
the scene's beauty settling back into place.

Ladders

That morning spent
  six feet
   from the ground,
    eight rungs up
     centring and ballasting him,
    precarious three and a half
    stories up,
     and reaching ever higher
     to the gutter-ridge,
     balancing the tools
     on the top rungs,
     the ladder shifting
     and bouncing
      on the stark wall,
      however I tried
      to ballast it
      otherwise.

      Those earlier
      mornings, me
      scrambled to the top
      of the slide, head of
     a shouting gang,
     children pyramiding
     the ladder below;
     only to lose nerve,
    fall to tears
    till someone's mother
    carried me down
    from what felt like
    the unsteady sky.

Riverrun, Cockermouth

for Paul Whitty

You disappear over the edge
of the muddy riverbank,
me fearful for you,
for the expensive recording
equipment, hydrophone,
headphones, microphone.
The day stalls, river's constant
sizzle across the little reef
of pebbles runs
between the banks,
one sectioned concrete,
the other, where we are,
nettles, grass, trees that might
already have stood
when he was born in the terracotta
house, walked the
terrace walk above us
a child crying laughing singing,
children laughing shouting now
by the Vets' Centre opposite
as they carouse the swings,
footballing the grass
against a dilapidated brick hut,
pushchairs and pensioners
clanking across the
wrought flaked bridge,
planes for ever processing
the muddied clouds over-head;
runs,
and the wind modulates
the flow over pebbles,
then leaves it back where it belongs,

332 metres per second
sounding
then rising away,
losing force,
slowing to
34 metres per second
beyond the atmosphere
gradually, lingering,
following all the before noises
dwelling out there,
the previous sounds,
the sound of his voice

July 20th 1969

The white slats of the beach chalets
gleamed that sun-stunned day; short sand paths
to their steps showed muddled footprints,
all the family scampering
for the relief of Jaywick's waves,
with the beach scalding at our soles.

Crouched against warm wood, my trunks wet,
I watched worried as Dad fretted
at the coat-hanger aerial,
trying to steady the picture
that kept spinning off the screen's side.

Everything was paused, the beach-noise
seemed shuttered thousands of miles off,
as the TV briefly settled
into focus: the first foot felt

for the ladder-step, the fine grains
of dry sea-bed loomed ghostly below.

Friday Woods

Each early winter
we'd brave rain and wind
whining in tree-tops
to forage the mould
for bright green prickly

unsplit chestnut shells,
which we stamped down on
to open a gash,
and, with hurt fingers,
hooked out the sheened nubs.

Better, though, to hunt for
a short heavy stick
to hurl at branches
where bunches of spiked
husks gleamed light against

rain-darkened fanned leaves,
then to duck and run
as chestnuts and stick
plunged back toward us
from storm-rushing skies;

better still, though, to
stand where you were stood
as the load thumps near,
face up to cascades
of icy droplets.

From a Canal Bench

Why stay patient at
the droplet-fall
of sap beneath this beech,
small, speckled spiders
lowering on their threads,
floated snippets of blossom,
minute green beetles
and weighty black flies
settling on the bench-planks?

The digger crunches on
across the distance,
its hod juddering up soil,
beeping steadily at
its reverses. Trains
grind nearby tracks.
Aphids, thistledown,
inescapable feather-fluff
floating from dandelion-clocks;

yet the branches
hold the clouds,
suffer the clouds
to wander beyond
the shrouding horizons.

Red Mason Bee

A skilful artist,
her fine ginger hairs
were her deft paint brush,
ever-yellowing
as she danced the air
dabbing pollen grains
pink blossom to pink
blossom, tree to tree.

The finger-nail sheen
inside snail shells glowed
as she layered rose
petals for her nest,
then laid an egg there,
bunged each shelter-hole
with chewed clots of soil,
all to incubate.

Stag Beetles

A reflection: that July day
spent hunkered down, banking up earth
around the celery stalks, say
when I was ten; hating Dad's laugh

at the time it took me to do.
I wrestled the two steel buckets
hotly to the compost heap, through
his pea-canes and currant bush nets.

Where I was shocked. On the heap's top
two huge stag beetles had locked horns –
a black circling that did not stop
at a boy's shadow which had torn

across their world. I'm sometimes scared
in dreams by their strange aggression:
that clack of horns memory once heard
now just sad imagination.

Kites at Wittenham Clumps

Everything had harmonised literally
that day your blue and yellow winged kite rose
immediately to its high extent
in the wind-shriven cloudless sky, and four
then five red kites riding thermals over
this ancient stand glided in around
and stayed there, inspecting your alien
irruption far-borne in the scene; till one,
in one fast pass, seemed about to attack
your kite or seize on it, before sheering
away back out over the sprawling array
of clashing-coloured sun-swamped fields and roads.

Medusas

The swim was a muse, a steady strong pace;
locking in thoughts, reflections across flat bay,
till one stroke raised a triple-Medusa-

bracelet of pain, brown foliage tentacle
wrapped up a forearm, thousand-needle jag
bringing the horizon lashing inwards,

whip-welts stone-nulled down the arm to this hand.
And, on the next swim, a sharp ache from yearning
tentacle-sores at their return to their sea.

Away

Two sparrows on the balcony-rail,
a gull on the buoy; arcs of silver-
glinting fish leaping from the sea,
plocks as they leave it, plocks as they return;
purple mimosa trailing over
white walls, the moonpath opening out
across the steady roll of the waves;
fishing boat lights beaming on then off
far out in the wide span of the bay;
scribbles of light on the flat sea-bed,
those silver fish swimming deep below;
weighty calm of a beach in sun –
hold it now, it within, hold it here.

'Yet With Time's Cycles Forests Swell'

If we kept in our minds
fishes' fins could be wings
raising all up into
a chemical soup sky;
or that a dull granite
boulder could shift with ice
the hundred miles from Shap
to Filey just like that –

or if we imagined
waking into bee-less
silences in spring-times,
worried what we would eat –

if only we'd conceived
of a fossil sepia
sketch of a dinosaur
in ink as old as it;
or if everywhere
raised cathedrals of light
and scope uplifting life,
showing us what life is –

if only we'd foreseen
that pesticides might flow
from fields and suffocate
Hughes's salmon and pike;
or known that reserpine
from shrubs reduces stress
and its rainforest homes
are already half gone –

if we'd seen razorbills
surfboarding on branches
to behead frogs downstream;
or a Cleopatra
flexing yellow wingtips
and raising itself to
blue Banbarian skies
like a coloured flick book –

or we'd understood that
whatever in a day
comes into being dies
from the world that same day –

maybe we'd change our thoughts.
Maybe we would think.

The Dying of Orpheus

after Ovid, *Metamorphoses* XI 15ff; V 48ff; VI 349; II 227; I 285; etc

the unnatural voices, clamour, the riot
the mother-of-all-bomb shatterings
the self-slapping and furies of the afflicted

the caterwaul as birds of day rip at
birds of night who have wandered out of time

(the tearing jet engines, motor bikes,
the constant drilling and mining and sirens)

bawl against natural consonance,
stutter persistent rhythm
cannot give it ear

    – so that:

    everything gets translated to extremes

    (algae darken the icecaps, absorb light,
    meltwaters and oceans heighten)

    too much sun, then violent rains
    perish and corrupt the crops,
    rampant darnels and thistles exhaust the land;

    water, which should be shared by all,
    is stolen for some; good air

    (power, gas, light)

    given for the life of all,
    is captured for the few

the nursing mother is parched
till her pharynx no longer wheezes into voice

the sun sets the world in all parts
ablaze, a vast furnace

(bushfires, forest-fires, prairie-fires wild-fires)

flaring air unbreathable
seas and lakes contract,
dust and sand accumulate,
lake-bottoms fissured as deep as Hell
are screened round the world

(reservoirs drain, Italy's
olives and grapes
desiccate on the bough)

till thunderheads gather again, bolts are thrown,
low fronts and winds unleashed
until all is sea (and tsunamis)
wolves, dolphins, sheep swim
among highest tree branches

(cars and advertising boards swept
along by river-race and overflow) –

beneath all the desire, forefends,
noise, news, tragedy

the singing travels,
ground bass threnody
constant
at the edge of hearing

Dedham Vale

Alone in that summer landscape,
trudging a crackalured grey path
between thick, tensed grasses along
the limit of the thin river,

willows tear pliant trails into
their dark reflections. Somewhere near
the ghost of a lark hovers high,
shrilling lost distress. Cumulus

billows soundlessly, breezes ruffle
the glassy surface as I strike
towards the field-gate, circling past
the thick lightning-struck trunk where once

I paused to hold someone close
in its shadow, and idle there,
in quiet to gaze the rough hedges
and shallow hills of a future.

Some Other Where

after Propertius, *Elegies*, IV.vii

Ghosts live, to some senses:
death doesn't inter all things
into a past. Some thing
shimmers freely beyond
cremation's flare of loss.

When our love dissipated,
and I'd lapsed into sleep
where my hand strayed over
to cold sheets where you'd lain,
still you seemed to lean
over the bed, hair, eyes,
as I recalled them.

Only your clothes' colour
was hard to bring back; the form
of the beryl ring I gave
distorted. I could no longer
shape my lips to your lips,

but your breath between them
and your voice were real,
as you made the night air
resonate, clicking frail
fingers on thumb-bones at me:

'Have you already dropped asleep
towards me, have our furtive
restless nights already faded
for you? or the times
we had *al fresco* sex,
moving together, bare

soil agitated beneath us?
forgotten love-words you gasped
which the wind shattered to noise?

Through dividing passageways
memories are wreaths laid
on this poisoned world-stream
where we all scull about
aimlessly.
      Along one bank,
shades, moments from the past
drag back intimate guilts.

On the other stream-bank
we're stolen away by flower-
scented images to the place
in our brains where we danced
to our song that time
in a sweltering Leeds night-club.

Plant ivy in that region
where you have settled me
in your mind; let the fullness
of its berries, dendriting tendrils,
preserve the wavering memory
of me.
      Picture us on
our river walks, meadows

and orchards, sunlit scenes
that will never fade away.
Don't let our happy daydreams
lapse; if they are good ones
they always mean something.

At night our thoughts stray
free of day's fore-shadowings,
but with dawn we return
to life's pale stale marsh, we
are translated to silence.

All the other lovers haunt,
but I'll hold you soon, body
to my body, some other where.'

Once your voice died away
your image rose, ungrasp-
able beyond my arms'
quick reach to embrace you.

II. The Valley of the Temples
A Fantasia

'...there are just these [elements]...
they become different things at different times
and yet [are] ever and always the same.'
— Empedocles, Frag. 349

'*24 April* [Sicily] – *Grigenti* All we can see out of this green and flowering land is the Temple of Concord... the other sacred ruins are invisible...

25 April At sunrise we were at last permitted to walk down the hill...through lush vegetation without stopping once. The ground beneath our feet was undulated like waves over the hidden ruins.'
— Goethe, *Journey to Italy*, translated by W.H. Auden and Elizabeth Mayer

'...fixos oculos
aversa tenebat...'

'...stayed turned away
face set...'
— Virgil, *Aeneid* VI

Elements

The path is inevitable, a cobbled way
stretching straight past wrecked temples. Each in turn
is to be visited, as they grant look
and outlook, rising on successive rock-crests
by the path and focusing the skyline.

Fallen limestone columns, crumbled pediments,
entablatures which have ripped over
tympana and wrenched roofs from rooms and cells,
membranes through which the gods escaped away –

when the gods went free, we,
exiles, turned from our selves

*

SPHERE

VORTEX

STRIFE

LOVE

VORTEX

STRIFE

HARMONY

VORTEX

DISCORD

SPHERE

*

sayer of the not-to-be-said,

soul barer...

dowser of spirit-secrets...

player dabbling humans and gods:

interference, Twitter-alerts,
cacophony, invest the air:

tauten, sound the slacked strings,
lend them tone-traces again

(After Hölderlin)

Agrigento, Sicily

I.

Yellow-brown rock-dust
wirelesses
sun-glare
through the eye
on the steep climb
to the temple plateau,
from where

awe spans,
ghosts of wave-falls
lulling through
wind-breaths

II.

Moon is framed
between pillars,
the apogee
bringing lost sea

to temple-plinth
sanctum-spaces
awaiting dawnlight
to grip the initiate-path

(rosemary and jasmine)

clumps of cobbles awkward
beneath passed
and expectant feet,
the footprints leavings
in shell-tufa

III.

Sun and moon
too much for the eye
however framed, lured,
harboured:

pupil
flinches at their weight,
iris retracts,
stalls in flight scoping

(rosemary and jasmine)

god-shadowed
tree-glades
of ridged beige stone

IV.

And the descent,
the grave path
into the orange grove,
its laden trees, then,

in the depth of the gorge,
the cave-groove
in the cliff-face,
(entomb-space,)

sherds, pebbles
scattering the rock floor;

pause and absence
sheltering from
concentrating sun

Two lovers pore over the official guidebook for Sicily, Agrigento: The Valley of the Temples and Surroundings. *Its opening section on 'the fascination of the past' tells them that, after defeating Carthage in 420 BCE, the ancient city flourished; there was, in the awkwardly translated phrase, 'a building boom which led to the realization of the magnificent ensemble of works of art which constitutes the Valley of the Temples', the string of huge buildings along a cliff-scarp which originally faced the sea at the edge of the city. 'The great philosopher Empedocles lived and worked in the city'; Pythagoras, Pindar visited, before this 'golden age' was destroyed by a 'period of vicissitudes'.*

Through the long day of blinding heat, the lovers tramp the broad pathway past the temples with a scant crowd of other tourists, stopping at each shattered building to read their guide.

Because of the intense sun, because of their intent feeling for each other, the site shimmers with presences, with past figures who seem to displace those of the faces and dress of the modern tourists. At each stop, the lovers feel too their own past loves ghosting them, and each temple comes alive with the qualities and symbols of the gods to whom the building was dedicated. Each spot seems just left by joys and hurts, desires and desists, presences and lost ones shared between times. The traces and signals haver stronger and less strong; sometimes they command, sometimes they send silent images that concern and disconcert, or bring their own light and knowledges of the world.

Hera

'There is nothing intrinsic about the flowing of time'
— Carlo Rovelli, *The Order of Time*

I.

Processions along
the sacred way;
ones with tambours,
ones flaunting the thyrsus,

olives and loaves
in elbow-crooked
reed baskets,

(rucksacks with *panes*,
vacuum-packed cheese, bottles
of water in hands)

ones with bound sheaves
of ripe wheat waved
by shore breezes,

ones in priest's robes
following drum and flute
pacing danced

steps tracing
the temple-way,
mapping a path of songs

at noon,
hour of ghosts
that silent as shadows
on brick and stone

II.

That evening of sunlit cobbles,
our legs dangled over
the river-wall, when you said

everything had become dull,
no life or thought or desire
flowed out to each other

anymore, your attention had settled
elsewhere, and now we were locked jealously
in spiralling turmoils of loss,

all curled embryonically, love
retreated to monotonies
like this summer evening

where we always end

*

I have never strayed
further beyond myself
than
in our small rooms,

carillioning
bird notes startling
skylit air, the pent,
as light depicts

skin with sheens –
arms, backs,
chest, groin,
sprawled knees –

blackbirds, sparrows,
Demeter's turtle doves

III.

Who to turn to? What will be there, when
we look back? The voices again, flooding
the brain with ether-static wittering
saying about what might have been betrayed,
or what might demand monstrous attentions
in our ears' labyrinths. Tell me. Turn to me.

Am I to be
the subject, is this? are you? We woke to
the sigh of waves against the stark cliff-rock,
the dwelling of sun across azure seas.
Watch it glimmer there, sherds of night dancing
between wavelets; watch sandstone hillsides emerge
from mist the other side of the bay.

Unmask. Breathe. Hold you face up to light
reflecting from lime-washed walls. Cherish warmth
as day clarifies from the past yet turns nightwards.

Hawks through blue air, peacocks prancing
lush carpets of dittany, poppy, lily,
feather-eyes glinting, shimmering the sunlight.

Iris-iridescence might unite two
who in this moment hold each other
dear, bridge of colour grazing them until
they fade into plain day, lapsing back
as the dream breaks, and harmony discords.

What haunts us is the instant of distinct
rainbow fronting darkening skyscapes, yet also
the indistinct moment when colour drains from
the last-minute droplet, and relapses
beyond yearn of eye and mind to keep it there.

What haunts
is the disappearance of the hawk
over the last tree-top into winter dusk;
the recession of peacocks into shade
beneath hedgerows at the end of short days.
Poppy-light, dittany, grey; colour separates,
atoms of light float apart into dark.

In that moment love was lost forever;
as we moved to the light, the light pixelated.

The god-touched earth rests, threads of soul
stretch to limit. Iris pauses. Who to turn to?

Concordia

'The present has no meaning. "Now" means nothing'
— Rovelli

I.

As we clamber
the steep slope up
the rock plateau

I dream musics
that span ahead,
desires particulating

between us, shifting
resistances away,
enlivening eyes.

But your step
falters then stops
as you shy,

sounding
what it might
come to mean

as I turn
lost
my gilt head

to the
space now
lost of you

II.

All the buried moments,
missed holdings,
fears, diffidence,

senses of unworth –
all the turnings-away,
needed permissions, lonely

*

Emptiness at the heart
of all things, round all things,
time leaking sap
from the pattern,
the void seeping into mind:

when we undergo our blisses,
we meet again
what they have already felt
but fended from recall,

for I have already been
a boy and a girl,
hedgerow and a bird,
but most a leaping
journeying fish

*

We settled readily into a joyless place,
love like rennet clogging
air in that cold-stilled room,

where I said into silence
we were just survivors
clinging to our life-raft,

and you, tiredly,
'you can kiss me
if you want to.'

      *

Yet were it some ripple
or stretch
in the gravity-curtain,
or quirk of quanta
on the web-waves,

that, were some
coincidence
to occur some
other where,

a grain of
you might touch past
me gently
fifteen thousand
years from now,

I might feel and know
again your loving-kindness

III.

Exhalations
and effluences
of all rainbow colours,

from dawning earth
into ether
turning radiant heat.

Eris is absent,
but shuttered
behind the ultramarine

a storm
sheds hailstones
like golden apples

through sun-bright
in a spill
of atom-seeds,

particles of earth
and air, fire, water,
rhizoming, globing.

What fruits do we gather
from the underworld, or ones
reached high from autumn branches?

In your left hand a goblet,
turned Welsh pottery,
in your right a wood platter

with cornucopia of berries
of the season and out
of season. Bind, gods,

our bodies close
for ever
at this intersection

of their strength
and pliance.
But harbour us,

enclose us in that labyrinth
where we cannot know ourselves,
knowing who to turn to.

To harbour lovers
in the house, to nurture
their loves and them,

here where there
is no settled place,
roof-fallen pilgrimage.

Herakles

'We are histories of ourselves'
— Rovelli

I.

A figure seems
to flit between

the giant stones,
cupping careful

hands round the flame
in a boat-shaped

lantern, breeze-ghosts
threatening it;

the figure's bare
foot feeling each

step a launch into
trial, uncertainty,

passing fallen
columns, sheered blocks

within this shade
from dense carob-trees

II.

We carried each other
two hard winters, our times
together by coal-fires
or in bars, dreaming together
through cold nights in your room,
brief amongst the missings;

your happier times teaching
far away, the heavy
wranglings shouted into
queued-for phones, letters with
faked fraught gestures of love.

*

You said we should meet beneath the heart window,
which I hadn't realised was a heart;

shivering in your long coat, stood there
in the snow, waiting to show me

within the vast arches of stained glass
was nestled that shape that expressed us

for you, who I could not bring back to warmth
after my flinch of scorn, however

I swaddled you with my arms, or kissed
frantically at your face and freezing mouth.

III.

Grass snake on the path,
a raven scraking
on the roof-ridge,
doom-scroll of star-blaze
at the horizon;

lightning flashes
translate dangerous
skies to earth
where temples
make the storm visible:

return the portent
to the signs,
reteach us
to read these things.

Blood on snow,
tears on a face,
trail of livid droplets
into thick forests.

It infects dreams.
It insinuates fevers
gasping heads, bodies
strugglingly turned on beds.

These nightmares
proliferate;
tell out one, it
hydras and hydras.

Where to find which temple
to lie down and take rest?
Grooved pillar-drums
slump at crazy angles,

huge limestone dice
thrown across
the temple-ridge by
transgressed gods.

Seek a sanctuary
graced by poplars,
and bed down as though
in a golden pill,

embryonic
to wait out vengeances.
Don't violate
the sacred things:

that tripod the Pythia
perches on above
the abyss, its vapours
from deeps of inspiration

don't struggle
it from under her,
to gain it yourself
and dictate the future

through drugged
syllablists' hexameters.
Burn what is mortal,
braise it infolded on the pyre.

What rises from the flame
is not winnowed ash,
but air-waved possibility
to be transumed by the gods.

Whatever moves
(moves us) is immortal.

Castor and Pollux

'We understand the world by studying change'
— Rovelli

I.

Columns, random stones
shapen and fallen;
light brings focus
to what we know
and need, feeling

apart and at one.
Your finger bones
are visible
held against sun –
two parts earth, two

water, four fire
and insoles, pale
white forms shining
from scumbled lost
masterpieces

II.

That evening of wine,
sat on your hearth rug
before the coal fire,
whose shifting embers
cast a glow on your face
as you smiled and kissed

our future of evenings
of wine before
that sifting coal fire;

but my breath shortens,
heart empties, recalling
my coward's mistake,
believing our yearning
would always be there
for us to delight in
before the coal fire;

recalling your cold
fixed face, disappointment,
and our automaton-
awkwardness and chill
on the doorstep when
I lamely turned up
over a week later,
having missed that moment

you meant
and yearned for,
that evening of desire

before now unlit ash,
hopes and love heated to glass.

III.

They meet at a right angle,
two pillars to each side
stock on a chunky platform

upholding frieze blocks
into shifting skies,
entablature jointed;

*Only in relation
do we know where we are
unknown to all others.*

*The one there, the other
out of sight, below ground.
The one rises, the other sets.*
Buried, the other's body
marks the land,
boundaries scope for its other.

Amphorae of ash and bone,
necks above ground,
punctuate hillsides, are danced by.

Can you catch
the voices
breathed from within

speaking words
that will not translate
(key their modal song)?

Strange how the
wings whirred overhead
seem to pump
cries from the arrowed beaks
with each beat.

Born from one egg,
warmed beneath white feathers
in a high nest of reeds,

they yet circulate,
the one knowing the other's
appearance its own darkness,

bright amid the boundlessness
and wilderness of seas.

The Chthonic Gods and Demeter's Spring

'The Earth slows time in its vicinity'
— Rovelli

I.

All the past just below:
tear up pavement slabs,
the bones couched there are
foetally-clenched,
kindly arrayed.

Make pause at the step
to edge of top step,
then two quick strides down
across the next two,

you who step along,
then pause again on
the low bottom step
down to the dancefloor

shivering, fearful
in the endless dark
waiting for your god
to be shown through fire:

we are panpsychics
who cannot think
the gods close.

II.

That greeting-you from the train
when you came back to me,
the trunk, heavy cases

wrestled from the trolley
into the taxi,
then joy and love

amongst suitcases broadcasted
around in your room;
but you still far away

from me, we resenting
closeness and lives given up
those lovely days and nights

where everything stayed packed,
belongings ready to go back,
whatever longings enacted there

*

Both there and here,
to come, then, now,

wielding words, wilding them

htere,
nthowen, nmcotoe
temoonwthnec,

grains skittering,
re-melding,
effluxing, emanating
prospects, step, step,

epts, tpse,
visual, verbal, aural,
wireless-waved
l-, l-, l-

    *

to touch you
one more time
to will touched is
I will have been touched
was touched in future
will be in past,
willed tomorrow,
was touched tomorrow,
will be yesterday,
now not, now not,
touch now

enjamb
me, re-
articulate
elbows, knees,
wrists, ankles
no syntax
just at once re-
lation
letter-by-letter
traipsing

III.

Frenzied
from lung-torturing
plunge through
the wooden labyrinth,
his brain groping for the map
to the self-created vortex,
its twists and gaps,
ox-foul blackness
swiftening and gaining;

agonising
loss in this escape,
the wax-drops
weeping then cascading
from the whirr of his son's wings
and drop body-shattering
(being so caught up
by sun-flares)
on translucent waves

yet he soared and circled
as he arrived over beauty
at this spot, its calm
river, living spring
echoing to itself
in myrtle-sprouting rock pools.

Gods of underearth
rest waiting,
breathing,
Demeter, Persephone
chasmed beneath earth;
spill wine to call them

pacing to silent music
till the tympanum,
Demeter, Persephone,
reawakens.

The water pouring from crusting rock
burns icily in summer heat, salves the heart,
before it drops into ages-smoothed basins.

Unceasing harvest, even when cold mist
plumes up the mountainside, returns as clouds
to chill hibiscus-draped and stepped cliff paths.

The wheat stands golden across hillside fields,
sensing each hush of breeze, feeling each shift
in Sicilian weather.

                        But something might fall
away, some storm blasted from Etna's slopes
flatten the corn, lay asphodels beaten

into yellow-brown mud. The god will be
absent again, searching and pleading
again for a lost daughter, disappeared
again for two seasons from this world.

Then water flows once more, initiates
find their way along the path of song,
the blank stones of the mysteries clash back
once more and resound across river reeds.

And the griefs continue, harvests fail,
the gulf stream veers unpredictably astray
following a god who wanders seaways
and shore-plain beneath the ridged temple-scarp,

awaiting a keying glimpse before love
is stolen back beneath the undulated ground.

Gods are in
the atom-seeds

Turn, turn…think fit to look upon my happiness.

Recognition

They see that from the shell-tufa
between cobble-slabs,

as the shadow of plinths
and few upright columns

passes twice daily,
grows the woody stem

and warping arms
of sea-dew rosemary.

Cicadas, humans
so in love with the singing

they wane to tymbals,
admire the Cleopatra butterfly

resting on its leaves, yellow wings
flexing in sun, transmitting

earth-sphere's lapse again
swirling to underworlds

The Way Across

from Aeneid VI, passim

this crowding
        of the destitute, ungraved,

circulates the shore
        and will find no way across

the raucous vortex of waters
        until their bones are set to rest, o gods

*

not far away the mourning fields where
        shades harsh love withered

cower behind myrtle-groves;
        at death

memories and missed moments
        plague, eyes turned fixed away

*

…among asphodels…

*

calm summertime,
        bee-lit meadows

humming multitudinous
        with flowers

*

electric seeds of life
    when unhindered by metastasis,

untethered
  by this globe,

escape
    from lovely bodies deathful

     *

let my hands release
    purple lily petals

let me range widely
    scopes of opened air

Two Rivers Press has been publishing in and about Reading
since 1994. Founded by the artist Peter Hay (1951–2003),
the press continues to delight readers, local and further afield,
with its varied list of individually designed,
thought-provoking books.